MARY, THE MEDIATRIX OF GOD'S GRACE

MY CALL TO THE ROMAN CATHOLIC PRIESTHOOD AN AUTOBIOGRAPHY

Revised Edition

by

Rev. Fr. Evaristus Uche Obikwelu

MARY, THE MEDIATRIX OF GOD'S GRACE
My Call to the Roman Catholic Priesthood
An Autobiography
Revised Edition

By

Rev. Fr. Evaristus Uche Obikwelu

Published On this Day, Saturday May 13, 2017
The Hundred (100) Years Anniversary
of the Apparition of Our Lady of Fatima in Portugal

Copyright 2017 © Evaristus Uche Obikwelu

All Rights Reserved. No part of this publication may be reproduced, stored in a retrieval system, or transmitted in any form or by any means, electronic, mechanical, photocopying, recording or otherwise without the prior written permission of the copyright owner.

Visit us at
www.fruchemarybook.org

**Dedicated to my
MOM**

Georgina Udenwa Obikwelu, (Image Date 1964)
"When one cultivates in the Lord's vineyard,
the Lord cultivates in his."
- my mom

*Unless otherwise noted,
all pictures are from the author's personal collection.*

Mary, the Mediatrix of God's Grace

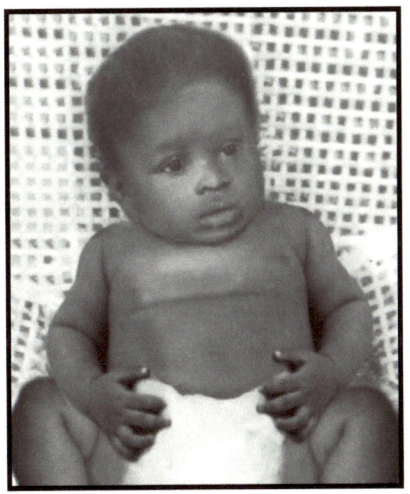

Uche as a baby

Mary, the Mediatrix of God's Grace

CONTENTS

Foreword 1
Introduction 3
Preface 7

Part I: FORMATION AND ORIENTATION
Chapter 1: Irish Missionaries 13
Chapter 2: Papa and Mama 15
Chapter 3: The City: Onitsha 21
Chapter 4: Block Rosary Crusade 23
Chapter 5: Altar Server 27

Part II: DISCERNMENT
Chapter 6: Life in Lagos 39
Chapter 7: Covenant with the Blessed Virgin Mary 43
Chapter 8: Europe Bound - Leuven, Belgium 55
Chapter 9: Life as a Student in Belgium 57
Chapter 10: Germany 61

Part III: MARY, THE MEDIATRIX OF GOD'S GRACE
Chapter 11: The America I Love 67
Chapter 12: Culture Shock 73
Chapter 13: Saint Mary Seminary 77
Chapter 14: Priestly Ordination 81
Chapter 15: Priestly Ministry 85

Part IV: THE BLASPHEMY OF OUR TIME
Chapter 16: The Havoc of Mary's Blasphemy 99
Chapter 17: Mary Versus World Celebrities 105
Chapter 18: The Silence of Goodwill 109
Chapter 19: 100 Years of Fatima Apparition 111
Chapter 20: The Mother of God Still Stands Tall 127

Acknowledgements 133
Reader's Comments 135

Mary, the Mediatrix of God's Grace

FORWARD

Father Evaristus Uche Obikwelu has written this very insightful and certainly interesting story of his call to the Catholic Priesthood. It has not always been common in the Nigerian-African culture that someone writes his own autobiography, but that's Father Evaristus (better known by his middle name, Father Uche) for you. Those who know him well, know he is outspoken, frank, to the point, but understanding, friendly and a people's person. All this he has laid out in this book. Father Uche has nothing to hide but rather is happy with who he is, his aspirations in life, his love of his native Nigeria and now, his love of the United States, his other home away from home.

He makes a strong point about how his strong Catholic family background has served him through his journey in quest of his dream and vocation to the Priesthood. It certainly has not been an easy journey, but his faith in God and devotion to the Mother of God has carried him so far, and continues to be inspirational for him in his priestly life and ministry. Those of us who know Fr Uche agree with him that his big smile comes off as an open mirror to the largeness of his heart. Fr Uche's smile tells of a happy priest. This autobiography is testimony that all is possible for one who has Faith.

Very Reverend Matthew C. Iwuji, JUD

Mary, the Mediatrix of God's Grace

INTRODUCTION
The Man
Reverend Father Uche Evaristus Obikwelu

I was born in Agulu, a town in Anambra State, located in the southeastern part of Nigeria. My family still lives in Nigeria. Pius Ifem Obikwelu, my father, died May 29, 2014, on the Solemnity of the Ascension of the Lord. Georgina Udenwa Obikwelu, his widow, is my precious mother. I have three brothers: Ilo, Father Chuks, Ndu, (deceased December 2014); and four sisters, Nne, Ify, Ngoo, and Ogoo (deceased 1972). I am the youngest of the remaining six children. There are many nephews and nieces in the family.

(L to R) Ndu (Late), Nne, Ilo, Uche, Ify, Chuks, Ngoo

# Rev. Fr. Evaristus Uche Obikwelu

My elementary and high school educations were received in Nigeria. Later, I obtained a Bachelor's Degree in philosophy from the Seat of Wisdom Seminary, also in Nigeria.

I am a cradle Catholic, coming from a strong Catholic Family tradition. Being an altar server in my youth initiated my deep interest and admiration for the priesthood. My mother took me to daily Mass and always encouraged me to participate actively in prayers, both at home and in the Church. All those prayers helped me immensely to discern becoming a Catholic priest.

In 2002, I left Nigeria on what would become my journey to the priesthood. I studied at the Catholic University in Leuven, Belgium, before moving to the United States in 2004. In America I became a seminarian in the Diocese of Austin. Saint Albert the Great Parish, in Austin, Texas, was my home parish.

When I was accepted as a seminarian by then Bishop Gregory Aymond, I began an eventful period of study and prayer. First, I went to Saint Mary's Seminary in Houston, Texas, for university level studies. Next, as part of my formation, I went to Cuernavaca, Mexico, to learn Spanish in the summer of 2005. In 2006, I served my Pastoral Year at Saint Mary's Catholic Church in Wimberley, Texas. That summer, I had Clinical Pastoral Education (CPE) at Hillcrest Hospital in Waco. Following that I studied at the Institute for Priestly

Mary, the Mediatrix of God's Grace

Formation (IPF) in Omaha, Nebraska, during the summer of 2007. I was ordained to the Order of Transitional Diaconate on May 17, 2008. I received a Bachelor's degree in Theology (STB), Master of Arts (MA), and Master of Divinity (M.Div.) from the University of Saint Thomas Aquinas, all in May 2009. My dream was realized when I was ordained to the Order of Priesthood on June 6, 2009.

My first official assignment was as the Parochial Vicar of Saint Vincent de Paul Parish in Austin, Texas, where I served from 2009 to 2011. On the second anniversary of my ordination to the priesthood, I was assigned as the Parochial Vicar of Saint Thomas Aquinas Catholic Church in College Station, Texas. Bishop Joe Vasquez appointed me the parish administrator of St Ann Catholic Church in Somerville, Texas, as well as its mission parish, Blessed Virgin Mary Catholic Church in Old Washington on the Brazos, Texas, on July 2, 2014.

If asked to capture my feelings about being a priest, my response would be, "I am joyful to be a Catholic Priest!" And to whom do I dedicate my vocation? My answer is, "To Our Blessed Mother, the Virgin Mary." I am currently happy and excited to serve in the Somerville and Old Washington parishes.

I have been privileged to serve in the following capacities: member of the Presbyteral Council of the Catholic Diocese of Austin, Texas;

 # Rev. Fr. Evaristus Uche Obikwelu

spiritual director of the Eastern Council of Catholic Women; and spiritual director of Red-C Catholic Radio in College Station, Texas. I enjoy posting reflections on the Church's teachings on Facebook, and write a reflection every Sunday in the Pastor's Corner of our parish bulletin.

My journey to the priesthood has been eventful, with many twists and turns. The Blessed Virgin Mary has been with me at every bend in the road. To honor her and to give credit where it is due, I decided to tell our story.

God Bless you all!

Mary, the Mediatrix of God's Grace

PREFACE
British Colony's 1914 Decision

The amalgamation of the Southern Protectorate and Northern Protectorate of Nigeria by the British Colonial Head, Lord Frederick Lugard, in my opinion, was a mistake. (Lord Lugard's wife, Lady Lugard, formerly Flora Shaw, coined the name Nigeria after the Niger River.) The British placed their economic and imperialist

Rev. Fr. Evaristus Uche Obikwelu

interests above the religious and cultural interests of the major ethnic groups of the country known today as Nigeria, namely, the Igbos in the southeast, the Yorubas in the southwest, and the Hausas/Fulanis in the north. The Igbos are Christians. The Yorubas were mostly Christians, with a small percentage of Muslims. The Hausas/Fulanis tribes were mostly Muslim, with a sprinkling of Christians and a few pagans.

In both the southeast and the southwest, the British had direct rule through warrant officers, who were selected by the British from the local populace. The warrant officer spoke both English and the native language so he could communicate easily with indigenous people. His authority superseded that of the ruler or the king of that particular area. Using a warrant officer to govern the local people is called Direct Rule. Direct rule in the southeast and southwest was easy to impose because most of the people from these areas received a western education from the missionaries quite early. They understood and spoke English, therefore, could communicate with the colonists.

However, in the north, were the Hausas, who were primarily a pagan people. During the jihad led by Usman Dan Fodio, an Arab named Fulani, came with his caravan and soldiers from the northern Sahara Desert to the southern part of the Sahara. Fulani conquered the northern part of Nigeria. He forced the indigenous Hausas to

Mary, the Mediatrix of God's Grace

convert to Islam and then imposed the Caliphate in the north, which headquartered in Sokoto. The head of the Caliphate is a sultan. The Sultan of Sokoto imposed the Sharia Law (Law of the Koran) in the whole northern part of Nigeria. They intermarried and the natives converted to Islam. In this way the sultan was able to implement the rule of his religion over the cultural rule of the people throughout the northern area. It was this system that the British encountered when they went to the north.

After the British presence was firmly established in the Southern Protectorate (made up of southwestern and southeastern Nigeria), the colonists decided to move northward to do the same thing. They met the resistance of the strong administrative and highly technical governance already in place in the north under the sultan's rule. Resistance made it difficult for the British to penetrate into the governance of the north. The British cleverly dealt with the sultan's government. Instead of fighting the northern people and wasting resources, they convinced the sultan and the other leaders that they could govern together peacefully. The British rule would be implemented through the sultan's existing structure of governance, in other words, Indirect Rule. Northern leaders agreed to this cooperative government but rejected the parts of western civilization that would change their religious way of life.

Two sets of rules existed within the same country. The Northern

Rev. Fr. Evaristus Uche Obikwelu

Protectorate operated under Indirect Rule, while the Southern Protectorate was under Direct Rule.

Mary, the Mediatrix of God's Grace

Part I:
FORMATION AND ORIENTATION

Mary, the Mediatrix of God's Grace

CHAPTER 1
Irish Missionaries

Around 1884 different European countries were exploring the African continent. The government of Great Britain, which was the dominant foreign country in West Africa, worked hard to establish its military presence. During the same period British Missionaries brought the Anglican Church (Episcopalian) to Africa. The Roman Catholic Church in the southeastern part of Nigeria owes a great deal to the Irish Missionaries who went there. These missionaries did their best to convert the locals to the faith they brought to the area. I would like to limit my reminiscences to the Catholic Missionaries and the faith they brought to my people, the Igbos.

Before the arrival of these missionaries my grandparents were non-Christians. However, they were a very spiritual and religious people. The Igbo culture, fundamentally, is known for its religiosity. Their chief priest, acting on behalf of the people, offered animal sacrifices to their god known by the names Chi, Chukwu, or Nna, which means God, Lord, or Father. Although they did not believe in a Christian God at that time, they believed that if somebody stole a neighbor's property, that person acted against Chukwu. If somebody helped a neighbor that person pleased Chukwu and would be rewarded by him. Their lives and daily activities reflected religiosity. For example,

 **Rev. Fr. Evaristus Uche Obikwelu**

their devotion was reflected in the names given to their children. My name is Uchenna, which means "mind of God" or "wisdom of God". One of my sister's name is Ngozichukwuka, which means "God's blessing is greatest". Such was the religious nature of the tribe of the Igbo race from which my family came.

When the Catholic Church finally began to make inroads into the Igbo land, it was easy for the native people to accept the God of Christianity, whom the Irish Missionaries brought, because the Igbo already had a very clear concept of a transcendental god or being. Hence, my grandparents did not object when my parents were baptized into the Catholic faith.

I believe that after the Philippines and Mexico, the Igbos of Southeastern Nigeria have the third largest number of vocations to the Catholic Priesthood in the world.

Mary, the Mediatrix of God's Grace

CHAPTER 2
Papa and Mama

Marriage, in many cultures, is a very important social phenomenon that plays a vital role in procreation of human beings. (Genesis 5:2) My parents came from a big town, Agulu, in Anaocha Local Government Area of Anambra State. There were twenty villages in the Town of Agulu, and my parents hailed from the Amoji Village. Papa joined the Nigerian Army on June 2, 1945. He was a dedicated and highly disciplined soldier, making it possible for him to rise in rank. Having achieved success in the Army, Papa felt the time was right to settle down. So, my dad, Pius Ifem Obikwelu, a young military officer, returned home to Onitsha to seek the hand of Miss Georgina Udenwa Moneme. My mom was a strong Catholic, devoted

Captain Pius Ifem Obikwelu

Ifem and Georgina Obikwelu on their wedding day, Onitsha, February 14, 1953

Rev. Fr. Evaristus Uche Obikwelu

to the Blessed Virgin Mary. After she lost her father, she left her mother in the care of her younger siblings in order to provide care for an aunt and uncle in Onitsha. That is where Ifem found her.

They observed all the traditional marriage rites and were happily married on February 14, 1953 (Valentine's Day). Their marriage was blessed with eight children, four boys and four girls. The boys are Iloegbunam (Ilo), Chukwudolue (Chuks, who is a Roman Catholic priest), the late Ndubuisi (Ndu), and myself. The girls are Nnemeka (Nne), Ifeomachukwu (Ify), Ngozichukwuka (Ngoo), and the late Ogochukwu (Ogoo).

Nigerian/Biafran War – The pogrom

The Nigerian Civil War, also known as the Biafran War, July 6, 1967 – January 15, 1970, was a war fought to counter the secession of Biafra from Nigeria.

On January 5, 1966, while my dad was serving as an Army officer in Lagos (then the capital of Nigeria, located in the southwestern part of the country), there was a

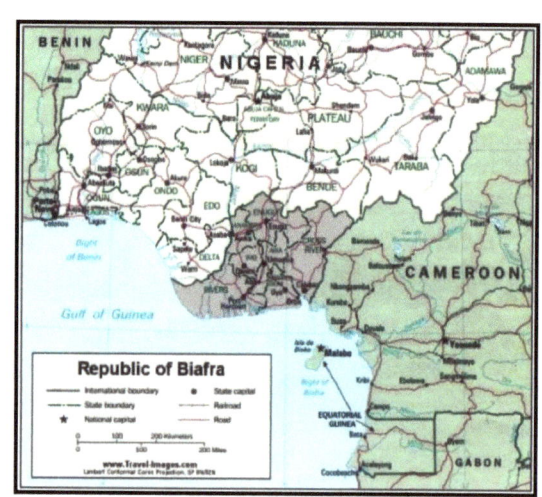

Mary, the Mediatrix of God's Grace

military coup by five young majors. Major Chukwuma Nzogwu led the coup, which resulted in the death of some politicians, especially northern politicians, including friends of my father. Mom said it was Divine Providence that my dad was on two months leave during the coup. She attributed the Godly coincidence to the intercession of the Blessed Virgin Mary. After the coup there was a quiet time. When Dad returned to his duties in Lagos, he was told by his commanding officer, General Murtala Muhammed, "You were a lucky man to be on leave all this while, otherwise, there was no way you could not have been involved in the coup since you were WO1 (Warrant Officer 1) in charge of signals." (General Muhammed later became the Nigerian head of state on July 29, 1975.)

As a result of the coup, there was a reprisal against the Igbo soldiers and officers, because the northern soldiers believed that the majority of the coup plotters were from Southeastern Nigeria. My mother, who was always at Dad's side, advised and encouraged him to escape and move back to Onitsha, in the eastern part of Nigeria, from which we had come. My dad was a strong, stubborn, and gallant soldier. He found my mom's advice very difficult to accept because he believed General Mohammed was a good friend – someone who would not hurt him. But my mom was insistent. A Shrine to the Legion of Mary was prominently placed in our family sitting room. Mom prayed the rosary there daily, asking for the intercession of the Blessed Mother to her son, Jesus, on behalf of our family. She knew the consequences

Rev. Fr. Evaristus Uche Obikwelu

if her husband was killed. Not only would she be left a widow, but she knew it would be very difficult to rear her children without an income. Our family knew that Mom's daily praying of the rosary was instrumental in creating circumstances that saved my dad from slaughter during the coup.

Mom also sought the assistance of her Irish parish priest. The Catholic Father supported Mom by encouraging my dad to heed his wife's advice and escape the area. Finally, he was convinced. He listened to the words of wisdom and left. Later, when northern soldiers came looking for him during the reprisal, he was not to be found. He survived to have more children, including me.

My mother's brother, my uncle, a very fine soldier and a perfect gentleman, Staff Sergeant Peter Moneme, was among the millions who died in that war. The grief was unbearable for my mom because his body was never found.

As the pogrom raged on, the military governor of Southeastern Nigeria in 1967, Colonel Chukwuemeka Odumegwu Ojukwu, could no longer secure and guarantee the safety of the Igbo people who lived outside the southeastern territories. The killing of the Igbo officers and people, and the burning of their property in Northern Nigeria continued. After the Aburi Accord for Confederation collapsed, the governor was left with no other choice than to secede. Southeastern

Mary, the Mediatrix of God's Grace

Nigeria became the Republic of Biafra.

This did not sit well with the Nigerian government, so the federal government of Nigeria, led by General Yakubu Gowon, launched what was called a three-day police mission to quell the Biafran secessionists. But the three days lasted three years! Such was the resilience of the Igbo people. At the end of the Civil War in Nigeria, in 1970, the government of General Gowon declared "no victor, no vanquished."

On January 12, 1968, I was born in the midst of the war. Can you imagine what it means to be delivered in wartime? Children born during a civil war either survive or die. I survived.

Nigeria and the international community did not ask, "Why is it that from 1914-2015 (101 years) the union called Nigeria has not optimally realized the goal for which Britain meant it? Why is it that many events that led to the Biafran War are still present?" The war killed between 1.5 million – 3 million Igbos (genocide). Even now, Igbos in Southeastern Nigeria continue to demand self-determination and self-rule. A small percentage of people from the area, prejudiced by their economic and political interests, do not agree. My question is, "Why is it that this demand still remains?" Nigeria and the international community overlooked the plight of the Igbo people. The United Nations said that employing a referendum is the best way to determine the true nature of the Igbo's self-determination demand. However, when the Biafran people of the Southeastern States peacefully demonstrated, either in Biafran areas or in the capitals of the world, they were arrested or fired upon by police. Unfortunately, it seemed that economic and political interests always drove the decision of the international community.

Nigeria's oil is in the southeastern states. Decision-makers feared that Biafran independence from Nigeria would jeopardized their economic interests. Britain took pride in the fact that they created the most populous black nation in the world. People with cultural, religious, ethical, moral and political differences deserve the fundamental right to decide their political future. In this case, I pray the world hears this clarion call from the people of the southeastern part of Nigeria who seek self-governance.

Mary, the Mediatrix of God's Grace

CHAPTER 3
The City: Onitsha

At the end of the Biafran Civil War most Igbos returned to their hometowns and cities located within Southeastern Nigeria. My dad and mom rented a home on Oguta Road, Odoakpu-Onitsha, East Central State.

One of the miserable outcomes of the Biafran War was that every Biafran or Igbo person who had money in the bank was stripped of their funds. Each was given only twenty pounds as a punitive measure for fighting the war against Nigeria. So, the Igbo people had to start life again from scratch.

Igbos are called the "Jews of Africa" because they are very industrious, religious, enterprising, commercially talented, and determined to succeed in life, like the Jewish people. They began with the little they had and, within a short time, Onitsha became a modern city. There were high-rise buildings and much commerce. In fact, by the late 1970's and the early 1980's the City of Onitsha had become the largest commercial market in West Africa. Not only the Northerners and the Westerners of Nigeria bought goods and products in Onitsha, but the indigenous people of West Africa also came. Most of the Nigerian visitors to Onitsha at that time erroneously accused the

 ### Rev. Fr. Evaristus Uche Obikwelu

Nigerian Federal Government, who fought the war against the Igbos, of secretly compensating the Igbos for the hardships caused by the war. That, unfortunately, showed how ignorant they were of the Igbo tribe's determination to succeed in life.

Mary, the Mediatrix of God's Grace

CHAPTER 4
Block Rosary Crusade

Bishop Francis Arinze became the youngest Roman Catholic bishop in the world when he was consecrated on August 29, 1965, at the age of 32. He was named the coadjutor (automatic right to succession) to the Archbishop of Onitsha. He attended the final session of the Second Vatican Council that same year along with the 45-year-old Archbishop of Kraków, Karol Wojtyla, the future Pope John Paul II. Following the death of the Archbishop of Onitsha in February 1967, Arinze was appointed to the position on June 26, 1967. He was the first native African to head a diocese, succeeding Archbishop Charles Heerey, an Irish missionary. During my teens, Archbishop Arinze was the head of the Catholic Church in my archdiocese.

When my parents found a home on Oguta Road in Onitsha, they immediately located a parish of their own, Christ the King Parish, and became active members. Their children who had not received some of the Catholic Church Sacraments of Initiation, like the Sacrament of the Eucharist and the Sacrament of Confirmation, were enrolled in catechism classes. Mom was a very active member of the Catholic Women's Organization (CWO) and Dad belonged to the Catholic Men's Organization (CMO).

Rev. Fr. Evaristus Uche Obikwelu

My Mom (L) and V. V. I. Okoye (R), during her seminar at Christ the King Parish, Onitsha

Mary, the Mediatrix of God's Grace

There are many apparitions of our Blessed Mother in the world: Our Lady of Lourdes, Our Lady of Fatima, and Our Lady of Guadalupe, for example. However, most Catholics of Igbo extraction were accustomed to praying to God through the intercession of Our Lady of Fatima who appeared in Portugal. The Irish Missionaries were instrumental in introducing and familiarizing us with the Lady of Fatima. The apparition took place in 1917, the same year that Vladmir Lenin led a revolution against the Tsar's Dynasty in Russia and formed the Union of Soviet Socialist Republic. Our Blessed Mother asked the visionaries to pray for the conversion of Russia and she asked that Russia be consecrated to her. The devotion to Our Lady of Fatima spread like wildfire through Igbo towns, cities, and villages. We loved Our Blessed Lady.

A Block Rosary Crusade was implemented in Onitsha. Children, guided by young adults, gathered at a designated spot, called the Center, on each street in the city at 7:00 P.M. and prayed together. A framed print of Our Lady of Fatima was placed on an easel with candles on each side, in full view of everyone. The picture featured an artist's rendition of the Blessed Mother standing on a cloud above a native oak of Fatima with a crown of twelve stars and a halo on her head and a rosary hanging from her wrist. She looks down on the three young children, Francisco, Jacinta, and Lucia, who were witnesses to the apparition. We Igbo children took turns playing the role of the three visionaries. Each evening one boy and two girls led

Rev. Fr. Evaristus Uche Obikwelu

the rosary for all the other children gathered at the center. On many occasions, I was honored and privileged to lead the rosary at our very own Oguta Road Block Rosary Crusade Center. Hustling and bustling, car horns honking, and traffic around us did not deter us from focusing on the Mother of the Lord.

Our Lady of Fatima
(Image from public domain)

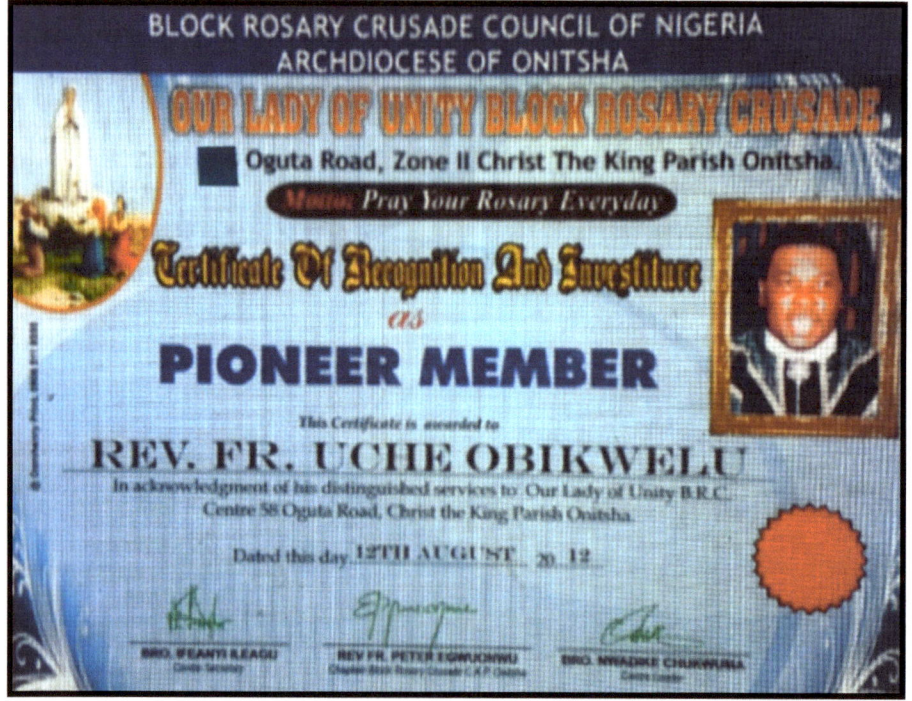

Certificate of Appreciation, Block Rosary Crusade

Mary, the Mediatrix of God's Grace

CHAPTER 5
Altar Server

Many young boys who were altar servers have gone on to take the entrance examination for the junior seminary, the equivalent of high school. The altar servers' ministry has been a major source of vocations to the priesthood in Igboland.

When I began to participate as an altar server, going to church with my mom and my siblings, I was registered in the catechism class (now called religious education in America). At the completion of the catechism course, students took an exam. I passed and was honored

Uche's Sacramental Record

Rev. Fr. Evaristus Uche Obikwelu

to receive my First Holy Communion. In 1978 I was privileged to be confirmed by His Grace, Archbishop Francis Arinze of the Onitsha Archdiocese. I was sponsored by Chief Aron Ozigbo.

When my mom took me to daily Mass, as early as 5:00 A.M., at Christ the King Parish, I often was the altar server. Consider waking up very early in the morning, being a child about six or seven years old. I was very sleepy sometimes. As an altar server I learned the names of the sacred linens, sacred vessels, and the different vestments that the priest wore to celebrate Mass. I was also involved in cleaning the sacristy and the altar. In a way these duties helped prepare me for being a responsible adult. Apart from the regular routine of doing all these tasks, I began to have a deep interest in the actions of the priest, both at the celebration of the Holy Eucharist as well as outside the church. Our priest went to the hospital to anoint the sick, witnessed marriages, baptized babies, and celebrated the funerals and anniversaries. When I witnessed and considered all these pastoral responsibilities, it became evident that my life, the life of my family, and the life of other parishioners, revolved around our parish, headed by our parish priest. I consciously began to develop a desire to be like my priest. I wanted to be a parish priest too.

I cannot put my finger on the exact moment I decided to become a priest, but, in retrospect, I can say there were many influences in my life. Attending the block rosary evening prayer, participating

Mary, the Mediatrix of God's Grace

in the family prayers that Mom always led before and after meals, before bedtime, and in the morning before we went to Mass, prepared me. Primarily, I credit my mom, who gave me motherly, spiritual leadership and encouragement, for my ultimate decision to become a priest. I requested the entrance form to Saint Dominic Seminary in Akpu, Anambra State -- a decision that started my journey to the priesthood.

I took the entrance examination. I passed. I was called for an interview and was accepted. After attending five years of high school at the junior seminary, I graduated with my West African Examination Certificate.

Uche, an altar server at age 7, peers into the future.

Pope John Paul II visited Nigeria in 1982

As a youngster I knew the pope rarely left the Vatican. Most people who visited Rome wanted to attend a papal audience. As an altar

 **Rev. Fr. Evaristus Uche Obikwelu**

server, being close to many parish priests, I understood that the pope was one of the reasons people made the pilgrimage to Rome. I vaguely understood the activities of the Second Vatican Council. Pope Paul VI was the first pope I remembered, because his portrait hung in the church sacristy and rectory of Christ the King Parish. After Pope Paul VI died, I saw his picture in the newspaper. A conclave then elected Pope John Paul I. I was troubled when I heard that he died shortly afterwards – just a little over one month after his election.

Next, Pope John Paul II (now St. John Paul II) was elected at the conclave of 1978. Immediately after his election I learned that Pope John Paul II wanted to travel outside the Vatican. I was really confused because I did not realize that the pope could be seen by everybody, not just a select few people. I was joyful at the news but, at the same time, I had mixed feelings. To me looking at the pope was the same as looking at Christ. The new pope's travels became world news. I quickly realized that a charismatic man had decided to take the faith and the word of Christ to the people of God – to the farthest ends of the world. Watching the pope's travels gave me goosebumps. He would alight from his plane, and the first thing he did was kiss the earth of the country he was visiting, a powerful sign suggesting he had come with the peace that comes from Christ.

I was in my second year at Saint Dominic Savio Junior Seminary when the pope came to Nigeria in February 1982. Since there were

Mary, the Mediatrix of God's Grace

many Catholics in the area, Onitsha was one of the cities the pope chose to visit. He held an outdoor Mass, and I was blessed to dress up and be one of the many altar servers in attendance. I recall wearing my red cassock with matching white surplice. It was an indescribable event that remains indelible on my mind. My desire to be a priest became stronger after that papal visit.

Pope John Paul II's visit to Nigeria in 1982
(Photo source: Information Nigeria)

Less than a year before the pope's visit to Nigeria an attempt was made on his life. I recall finding my mom crying in our sitting room. I asked her why she was so sad and downcast. Why were so many of our church friends mournful also? She replied that the pope had been shot in Saint Peter's Square in Rome. At that time, news did

Rev. Fr. Evaristus Uche Obikwelu

not travel as fast as it does today. Now information is instantly at one's fingertips. The color TV was just emerging and cable television was not in the home of every family in the world. It took a long time to get news from Rome. There was total confusion about whether or not the pope had been killed. Finally, we learned that the pope had undergone surgery and the bullets were removed. He survived the assassination attempt, which brought great joy and relief to everyone. To whom did the pope attribute his survival? Our Blessed Mother, the Virgin Mary, of course, the Lady of Fatima -- the same Lady of Fatima to whom we children prayed during the Block Rosary Crusade. The following quotation appeared in the press, "Death had appeared all but certain to bystanders when three bullets fired by Turkish gunman Mehmet Ali Agca tore through the pope's flesh on May 13, 1981. By John Paul II's assessment, 'It was a mother's hand that guided the bullet's path.' One of the bullets that struck John Paul II was later placed in the crown of the statue of the Blessed Virgin Mary at Fatima, Portugal."

I pondered how our Pope knew that the attempt to assassinate him was prevented by Our Blessed Mother. Of course, he was also devoted to the Lady of the Rosary. We have all seen the Pope depicted in the media, walking with a rosary in his hand. Pope John Paul II's example made a deep impression on me and affirmed what my mother had taught me about the power of the rosary.

Mary, the Mediatrix of God's Grace

After graduation, I was asked by Most Reverend Albert K. Obiefuna, the bishop of Awka Diocese, to go to the senior seminary, which is equivalent to college. There I studied philosophy and attained my Bachelor's Degree at Seat of Wisdom Major Seminary, an affiliate of Urban Pontifical University in Rome.

While we were in the senior seminary some of our professors, who had studied in either Europe or America, mentioned the decline in priesthood on these continents. I knew that Nigeria, especially the Igbo people of Southeastern Nigeria, were blessed with many vocations to the priesthood. For instance, my home Diocese of Awka had about forty seminarians. Thirty to forty seminarians were sent to Seat of Wisdom Seminary from each of the dioceses, so, there were two hundred plus seminarians in school at the time I was there. It dawned on me how beautiful and wonderful it would be if the Universal Church could share men with countries that had fewer vocations. That was when I had an "aha moment". For the first time, I knew I wanted to become a priest in America.

Uche enters Seat of Wisdom Seminary

Rev. Fr. Evaristus Uche Obikwelu

In the major seminary I was required to write a dissertation as partial fulfillment of the requirements to obtain my philosophy degree. I have a gentleman's knowledge of world events, like religion, politics, different ideologies and societal events. Suffice it to say that in the late 1980's I realized how dangerous Communism was to the Catholic faith in Russia, Europe, Africa, China, and around the world. I also knew that, in several apparitions, our Blessed Mother called for the conversion of Russia. Pope John Paul II did consecrate Russia to the Blessed Mother. So, I wrote "Atheistic Communism – Marxism-Leninism, A Critical Analysis". My philosophy professor, Reverend Father Dr. Jude Uwalaka, moderated my paper. I wrote about the danger of Karl Marx and his vision of a utopian, perfect society, which can really only exist in the world of ideas. Vladimir Lenin eventually brought the idea to practical implementation in Russia after the 1917 Revolution. For Communism to survive, religion must be destroyed. A common phrase in Karl Marx's book Das Kapital says, "Religion is the opium of the people." In my thesis I detailed why Communism is not only a danger to religion but also to the Catholic faith.

Uche in seminary, 1987

Mary, the Mediatrix of God's Grace

Agulu seminarians from the Awka Diocese, Uche second from right; late Bishop Albert Obiefuna in center. (1987)

In retrospect, I realized my paper was providentially motivated by Our Blessed Mother because, after I graduated in the late spring of 1991, the USSR was dissolved in December of the same year.

On a different note, it was, and still is, tradition that some seminarians, completing either their secondary school studies or their college seminary program, were asked to assist academia as teachers or administrators. After obtaining my philosophy degree, my bishop asked me to assist the academic faculty of Saint John Bosco Seminary, Isuaniocha, in Awka North Local Government of Anambra State. Interestingly, my older brother, Chuks Polycarp Obikwelu, was studying theology at the Bigard Memorial Seminary, Enugu State at that time.

After my one year assignment to the faculty, I took a break from

Rev. Fr. Evaristus Uche Obikwelu

the seminary to discern whether I wanted to continue on that path. During this period I attended the University of Nigeria in Nsukka, Enugu State, where I obtained a postgraduate diploma in public administration. Then, after graduation, I attended the National Youth Service Corps, a program designed to integrate different parts of the country after the civil war. I did my National Youth Service in Adamawa State in Northern Nigeria.

It is an Igbo societal reality that if you were not a Catholic priest or a reverend sister, you would, of course, have a family. During my Youth Service I had a girlfriend who was very intent on getting married. But I knew it was not the vocation for which God was calling me, so the relationship was discontinued.

Mary, the Mediatrix of God's Grace

Part II:

DISCERNMENT

Mary, the Mediatrix of God's Grace

CHAPTER 6
Life in Lagos

At the end of my service in the National Youth Service Corps, I moved to Lagos, the commercial capital of Nigeria. There I was thrown into the open labor market to fend for myself. I was welcomed by my brother Ndu's friend, Prince Kanu, who took me into his home. Cyriacus Uche Emebo was very helpful to me too, especially when I was preparing to travel to Europe.

I looked for jobs but secured only low-paying employment, such as the sales manager in a printing office and, later, the manager of a dry cleaning company. I credit my success in securing employment to the good will of Ifeanyi Achi. She ran a job locater service on the premises of our home parish in Lagos, Saint Leo Catholic Church in Ikeja, Lagos, and was very instrumental in helping me secure those positions.

At Saint Leo's I was a very active parishioner. I belonged to the Young Adult Catholic Association. I helped train the altar servers. I was a regular attendee at daily morning Mass, and at 3:00 P.M. every day, I attended the Divine Mercy prayer. I rose at 5:00 A.M. to go to Mass. The neighborhoods I walked through were often dangerous, so I walked in faith, praying the rosary as I traveled about one mile

Rev. Fr. Evaristus Uche Obikwelu

to services. The Blessed Mother protected me every day and I never found myself in jeopardy. Praying the rosary before Mass kept me in a very strong relationship with the Blessed Virgin Mary.

During these years I felt the urge to return to the seminary. I decided to find a way to go to America and become a priest there. I made a first attempt to go to America as a tourist, but the American Consulate in Lagos did not grant me a visa because I did not have enough money to sponsor myself.

In the meantime, my peers were getting married. Some were becoming successful in business and in their jobs. Some were not. However, I did not feel pressured to follow suit. Instead, I remained focused. I wanted to return to the seminary and, I hoped to become a priest in America. I wrote different dioceses and some universities in America, requesting admission. I wanted to go to America as a student or to be accepted as a seminarian in a diocese. Unfortunately, all my efforts were to no avail. I did not give up. I kept all my hopes and dreams to myself, but I presented them in prayer at Mass through my requests to the Blessed Virgin Mary to intercede for me. My parents were not aware of my intentions. My siblings were not aware, nor were my relatives and friends.

My brother, Father Chuks, was in Germany on an exchange program with the Archdiocese of Cologne. He returned to Onitsha on a

Mary, the Mediatrix of God's Grace

vacation but stopped to see me first in Lagos. After visiting the family, on his return to Germany, he stopped again in Lagos to visit with me a few days. During a conversation my brother broke some news from home that shattered my peace. What was that news? He said that during a discussion with my parents he learned that they were concerned because I was not getting any

Uche in Lagos

younger. They thought it was time for me to find a wife. Of course, my parents only wanted what was in my best interest. They wanted me to do as my age-mates did, that is, get married. I was shocked. I felt like I was between the devil and the deep blue sea because I did not want to get married, even though I honor and respect marriage. I had such a deep desire to be a priest. I really believed Our Blessed Mother would help make it possible. There was a ray of hope that brought peace to my heart when my brother, without knowing what I was thinking, told me that he had advised our parents to put the idea of Uche getting married on hold. He knew Uche was a very deep thinker, and he thought I might want to go back to the seminary. At that moment I opened up to my brother, confirming what he thought. I remember his beautiful smile and the amazement on his face. He gave me a big hug and said, "Uche that is wonderful!" He was truly happy for me. When he asked if I wanted to go to the

Rev. Fr. Evaristus Uche Obikwelu

seminary in Nigeria, I said no. Then he asked me if I wanted to go in Europe; I replied no. I told him I wanted to go to the United States of America. With concern, he remarked that our family did not have anyone there, neither friends nor family. His remark reminded me of John the Baptist's relatives. After he was born his mother Elizabeth named him John. The family told her that none of her relatives were named John. So, since I had no relatives in America, how could I go there? Well, I have a relative in the Virgin Mary!

Mary, the Mediatrix of God's Grace

CHAPTER 7
Covenant with the Blessed Virgin Mary

My parents' concern about my marital future conflicted with my internal desire to become a priest. The pressure became painful. I turned to my brother, Father Chuks, who advised me to visit my parents and talk to them, to let them know what I wanted in life. I did. My parents were satisfied and prayed for me, asking God to grant my heart's desire.

I returned to Lagos where I continued my everyday life, going to work and participating in church activities; but, this time around, I had a very clear vision of what I wanted. I realized that "Man proposes, and God disposes," but, when I considered the miracle of the wedding at Cana, I was hopeful. Jesus thought it was not time to perform a miracle. Nevertheless, He did so at the prompting of His mother. So my confidence in our Blessed Mother became firmer.

I began to pray in earnest. Whenever I attended Mass and the priest raised the bread of life and the chalice of salvation, I asked God to grant me, one day, the privilege of raising the bread and cup for Him on behalf of His people. I continued my devotion to the 3:00 P.M. Divine Mercy at Saint Leo Catholic Church in Ikeja, Lagos.

 # Rev. Fr. Evaristus Uche Obikwelu

One day I realized that the idea of becoming a priest did not actually emanate from me. I believe, instead, that it was infused into me by the Blessed Mother. Therefore, I decided to turn to the Mother of God for her intercession.

On the second floor of the priest's rectory at Saint Leo's, there was a chapel -- very serene and tranquil. Every evening precisely at 7:00 P.M. I went to this chapel, with my international passport in hand. I placed my passport beside the tabernacle. A statue of the Virgin Mary stood right next to the tabernacle and my passport. I prayed about an hour each time, listening for a message from the Virgin Mary. One day, during one of my regular visits, I decided to ask the Virgin Mary to make a covenant with me. I spoke to her as I gazed

I was the cross bearer at my brother, Father Chuk's, First Mass Madonna Parish, Agulu

Mary, the Mediatrix of God's Grace

Seminarians in casual attire – Uche (in center) with seminarians at Seat of Wisdom Seminary, Owerri

at her statue. "Mother of God, I would like to serve your Son as a Catholic priest. I would like to become His priest in the United States of America. I don't have anybody in America and I don't know who could help me go there either. What I do know is that you are the Mother of God as well as the daughter of God. So, since your Father and your Son created the people in America, I have somebody there -- someone I do not know. If you would help me go to America, to be accepted by a diocese or by a bishop, I shall commit myself to abide by the seminary formation and do my best to become a good priest." As a condition of the covenant I added, "If I enter into the seminary in America and discovered that life in America is more lucrative and has more opportunity to become comfortable and wealthier than life in Nigeria, and then changed my mind about becoming a priest -- to become a doctor, lawyer, or engineer instead -- let me not be successful!"

Rev. Fr. Evaristus Uche Obikwelu

Less than two months after this Marian Covenant, my brother, Father Chuks, called me from Germany and told me that he had secured admission for me to study for a Master's Degree in Philosophy at the Catholic University of Leuven, Belgium. I was so excited that I went to the chapel right away to thank Our Blessed Mother. I told her, "No one has ever come to you and asked for a need and left without being granted what he asked. Mother, I do not want to sound like Oliver Twist, who said he wanted more, but I did not want to go to Belgium. I wanted to go to the United States of America. But at the same time, I'll take what you gave me. Please let Belgium be a stepping stone to America."

**Life at Seat of Wisdom Seminary,
Owerri, Nigeria, 1988 – 1990**

Mary, the Mediatrix of God's Grace

Mom and Dad at my First Mass in Agulu, Nigeria, summer 2009, Saint Patrick Parish

# Rev. Fr. Evaristus Uche Obikwelu

Celebrating Holy Mass

Mary, the Mediatrix of God's Grace

Speaking at functions and giving homilies

Rev. Fr. Evaristus Uche Obikwelu

The Crucifix – Our Hope of Salvation

Red-C Catholic Radio, College Station, TX

Mary, the Mediatrix of God's Grace

Pope Francis

Pilgrimage to Rome with my priest classmates, Class of 2009, Saint Mary Seminary, Houston, TX

Rev. Fr. Evaristus Uche Obikwelu

Father Vincent Anyama and Me in Rome

Pope Francis' Wednesday Papal Audience
I took this picture inside Saint Peter's Basilica Square -- just 7 feet away from the Pope!

Mary, the Mediatrix of God's Grace

Preparing to lead our Class of 2009 priests in Mass at Saint Peter's Tomb, 2014

Mary, the Mediatrix of God's Grace

CHAPTER 8
Europe Bound - Leuven, Belgium

On the night of September 7, 2002, just four days before the first anniversary of September 11th, I was aboard a Lufthansa Airline jet, enroute to Belgium with a stopover in Germany. By September 8th I was breathing different air -- cool and breezy.

I registered in the Department of Philosophy. As I studied and worked, I did not lose sight of what the covenant with the Virgin Mary meant to me. I believed she would help me get to America. I continued to say my prayers and attend Sunday Mass. The academic structure and system in Leuven was so busy that it did not leave time for daily Mass.

I was not a seminarian there, but a lay student who wanted to become a seminarian. During my earlier education in Nigeria, we students learned about the Catholic University of Leuven from some of our professors, who had attended this great school. I was impressed by what I thought was a university with solid Catholic tradition and morals. When I got into the university I learned that the only thing that remained Catholic about the university was its name. Secularism and idealistic relativism had taken over the school. This environment bothered me and I realized I was in the wrong place. I began to develop a plan to get to the States.

Mary, the Mediatrix of God's Grace

CHAPTER 9
Life as a Student in Belgium

Life as a student in Europe was quite different from student life in Nigeria. I was privileged to receive a scholarship from my brother's friends, Herr Bernd and Frau Waltraud Soendgen, who lived in Germany. Of course, despite the scholarship I still had financial needs, so I washed plates in the cafeteria and picked apples and pears on nearby farms. With these odd jobs I was able to pay expenses, like my student health insurance. Until then I did not know what health insurance was.

One benefit of my health insurance was dental coverage. I went to see my dentist and, surprisingly, I had a good visit. He helped me to keep my teeth healthy and the insurance paid 80% of the expense. I paid only 20%. I thought that was a good deal.

Let me share an interesting story about my teeth. In Nigeria, before I was thirty years old, I had a lot of teeth problems. I had already lost three teeth: an incisor and two molars. Since dental care in Nigeria was poor, I worried about what would happen by the time I reached forty or fifty years of age. I went to the Blessed Virgin Mary pleading, "Mother of God, you know that no one comes to you with a request and goes without being heard. I beg you to help me to retain my

Rev. Fr. Evaristus Uche Obikwelu

teeth, otherwise, I'll become toothless before I am forty-five or fifty." A miracle is not only when a cripple walks or when we can drink in the desert. For me it was a big miracle to have my missing teeth implanted and my oral health secured.

So, when I went to a dentist in Belgium, who used a computer to examine my teeth, he determined which ones needed attention. I was given a better means to keep my teeth healthy. The plea I made earlier to our Blessed Mother flashed back in my memory. She had answered my request. My missing teeth were replaced with implants when I got to America. Today I can laugh with thirty-two teeth. My mouth is like open doors when I smile. That is what I call a miracle – grace obtained through the Mother of God!

Father Uche's new smile

I have many friends with whom I studied in Leuven and with whom I shared my Marian covenant experience. Many of them called me "Joseph the Dreamer", and said, "Are you the only one who can say

Mary, the Mediatrix of God's Grace

that your success thus far can be attributed to the Blessed Virgin Mary?" Some Nigerian schoolmates, with whom I shared the covenant story, sarcastically suggested that the experience might not be extraordinary, but I knew it was my covenant that got me to Belgium and was making differences in my life.

Mary, the Mediatrix of God's Grace

CHAPTER 10
Germany

Reverend Father Polycarp Chuks Obikwelu, my older brother, was involved in a missionary exchange program between the Catholic Diocese of Awka in Nigeria and the Catholic Archdiocese of Cologne in Germany. He performed pastoral duties in the diocese, and studied for his Ph.D. in African pastoral studies.

Some weekends I visited my brother and some of his friends, especially my benefactors, Herr Bernd and Frau Waltraud Soendgen Wachtberg from Deutschland. During my visits, we saw many places of interest in Germany. I especially enjoyed seeing the big cathedral in Cologne. On one of these weekends, as my brother and I were at dinner in the rectory, he brought up a discussion that would eventually lead to a big change in my life. My brother said to me, "Uche, I have a priesthood ordination invitation from a one-time young student of mine, who will be ordained a priest in Houston, U.S.A. in the spring of 2003. I am very busy with my classwork and my doctoral dissertation, which will make it very difficult for me to attend. Since you have been talking about your covenant with the Virgin Mary and your desire to go the United States, would you like me to ask him to send you an invitation letter so that you can represent me?" In amazement I responded, "Absolutely!!" So, I returned to Leuven with great joy

Rev. Fr. Evaristus Uche Obikwelu

in my heart. However, I was unsure of what would transpire at the American Consulate in Brussels. Within three weeks Father Cyriacus Onyejegbu, then a transitional deacon, sent me an invitation to attend his priestly ordination. Armed with this letter I began to make contacts with some dioceses in the United States: Diocese of Houston (now Archdiocese), Diocese of El Paso, Diocese of Austin, Diocese of Chicago, and a few others. Some of them responded to me, asking when I planned to be in the United States. I forwarded the dates

My older brother when he was Transitional Deacon Chuks (L) and me (R), 1987

of the ordination in Houston. With the necessary documents, I went to the American Embassy for a tourist visa interview. It was not an easy encounter because they wanted me to guarantee that I would come back to Leuven. I showed them my passport, with the stamps of my European travels, after all of which I had returned. At the end of my interview, I was told to pick up my tourist visa in two weeks. After I received my visa, the first person I greeted and thanked was the Virgin Mary.

Mary, the Mediatrix of God's Grace

The Priestly Silver Jubilee Ordination of

Rev. Fr. Dr. Polycarp Chuks Obikwelu

Ordained a Priest

by

Francis Cardinal Arinze

13th August, 1988

St. Patrick Cathedral Awka

Part III:
MARY, THE MEDIATRIX OF GOD'S GRACE

Mary, the Mediatrix of God's Grace

CHAPTER 11
The America I Love

As I boarded a flight to the United States of America I thought, "America, here comes Uche!" However, since I had not traveled outside Nigeria until I went to Europe, I could not even imagine how long the flight to America would be. I thought the two continents were close to each other. (Geography was not my strong suit at that time.) So, the flight took off and I expected to arrive in only a few hours. After about five hours, I looked up on the plane's flight monitor in front of me and the line depicting the trip showed we were not even halfway to the States. Everything was the first time for me, and everything was amazing. When I looked through the plane's window at the Atlantic Ocean I thought I was looking at an oil spill. The passenger by my side, a good fellow, told me that it was actually the Atlantic Ocean. I fell asleep and, when I woke, there were still four more hours to Newark, where I would transfer to another flight to Houston.

The long flight gave me time to think. I had a very personal, and emotional experience. Seeing the Atlantic, knowing that the plane was going hundreds of miles per hour, the historian in me wondered how my brothers and sisters who were sold into slavery were able to survive the journey from Africa to the New World under

 **Rev. Fr. Evaristus Uche Obikwelu**

horrible conditions and in chains. I compared that to my comfort on a nine-hour flight. I began to weep because, if I was anxious and concerned on my comfortable flight across the ocean, how much more uncomfortable and troubled were the slaves being taken from their homes in Africa?

After a four-hour layover in Newark, I boarded a flight to Houston -- another four-hour flight. Upon arrival at George Bush Intercontinental Airport I was surprised at how big the United States was. Most of my peers in Nigeria and I knew about America only from what we saw on television. I thought America was cold year round. (I must have seen only winter programs on television!) I left Europe under cool conditions, dressed in a hooded, padded, wool-lined leather jacket. When I entered the airport, the air conditioning kept me comfortable. But when I stepped outside, I was welcomed to Texas by a type of heat I had never before experienced! By the time my friend picked me up, I was stripped down to my under shirt. I asked him, "What is about this heat wave in America? I thought it was a cold country." The friend who picked me up had been my classmate in junior seminary in Nigeria. He jokingly told me, "When we were in the seminary, we talked about Hell. This is Hell!" I got the message right away. If I became a priest in this part of the world, I hoped I would survive the heat.

Americans think Africa is hot. Well, television has given an erroneous

Mary, the Mediatrix of God's Grace

impression about Africa too! Like the United States, Nigeria has different weather seasons. During the season that I traveled to the United States, it was very warm in Nigeria; however, it was windy and breezy. Nigerian summers cause folks to sweat, too, but it is not the burning heat like I felt in Houston.

Because I was on a tourist visa, my visit to America would be short. I began to contact all the dioceses that I had written earlier. My first contact was with the Archdiocese of Galveston-Houston, an interview which was very unsuccessful. I felt dejected. I went back to my hotel room and slumped into bed. Lying there, with my eyes closed, I said to the Blessed Virgin Mary, "You have brought me to America. Aren't you going to get me a diocese?" Then I went to sleep.

I rose in the evening. After saying my evening prayer, I checked my email. Lo and behold, there was an email from the vocation director of the Diocese of Austin, Father David Konderla! I remembered vividly what he wrote. "Uche, if I can recall you would be in Houston now, attending the ordination. If you are still interested, would you like to get a bus ticket to Austin? Let me know the day you're coming, and I'll have someone pick you up at the Greyhound Depot in Austin." I was encouraged when he told me that there were already two Nigerian seminarians in the diocese. One of them was Father James Ekeocha. (He was the first Nigerian priest, if not the first African, ordained in the Austin Diocese by Bishop Gregory Aymond in 2007. I was the

 **Rev. Fr. Evaristus Uche Obikwelu**

second in 2009.) My dejected spirit came back alive.

When I arrived in Austin I was taken to Borromeo House, the formation home in Austin. I was warmly welcomed by Father David and a group of seminarians who were preparing for the Institute for Priestly Formation (IPF) in Omaha, Nebraska that summer. After everyone left, Father David and I had a chat. He suggested that we meet the next morning for Mass and, after Mass, have a formal interview. We retired for the night.

When Father David celebrated Mass in the morning, he prayed for the guidance of the Holy Spirit regarding our upcoming discussion. We talked after Mass. He reviewed my documents, commenting that I had a very good record, one that would be very valuable in my effort to become a seminarian. He reminded me that our meeting was informal. Everything depended on the bishop's decision. He agreed to forward my application and my intent to the bishop. Father David told me to return to Belgium and, while in Belgium, to get a testimonial from my home bishop in Nigeria, Bishop Simon Okafor (late) in the Awka Diocese. He also needed letters of recommendation from the rector and a professor at Seat of Wisdom Seminary in Owerri. My parish priest at Christ the King Parish in Onitsha would have to send my baptismal certificate. After I provided the information, Father David said that I would be invited back for another discussion and, maybe, acceptance. "Make no mistake about

Mary, the Mediatrix of God's Grace

it. If you're not accepted, you're heading back home," he told me. I thanked Father David for his wonderful reception and hospitality and asked him to keep me in his prayers. Then I took a bus back to Houston, the beginning of my trip back to Brussels.

While in flight back to Belgium, I was both happy and anxious. The journey had begun, but the end was still far away. I gave thanks to Our Blessed Mother, not only for the successful first-time journey to the United States, but also for the opportunity to speak to and be well received by the vocation director of the Austin Diocese. I never doubted that the hand of Our Blessed Mother was directing me each step of the way.

Back in Leuven, Belgium, I focused on providing everything the Austin Diocese wanted, praying intensely to realize my dream. Scripture says, "The kingdom of heaven is like treasure hidden in a field. When a man found it, he hid it again, and then in his joy went and sold all he had and bought that field." (Matthew 13:44) When the necessary documents were received in Austin, Father David called me and said that I could return to the United States to continue my discernment. Like the parable, I left everything in Belgium and went to the Austin Diocese in the Lone Star State.

This time around, I arrived at Bergstrom International Airport in Austin, Texas. Father David picked me up and I began my journey

Rev. Fr. Evaristus Uche Obikwelu

through discernment. He advised me to choose a church for my home parish in the diocese. I chose Saint Albert the Great Parish in Austin, whose pastor was Reverend Father Isidore Ndagizimana.

Mary, the Mediatrix of God's Grace

CHAPTER 12
Culture Shock

The America I had dreamed about had some surprises for me. First of all, when we watched television in Nigeria, we saw pop culture, like musicians, including Michael Jackson, Lionel Richie, and Madonna. We saw James Bond movies and a few others. So, the first positive surprise I had was that America was not just what I saw on television. The churches were full, just like those in Nigeria. The priests were still respected, despite the scandals of 2000. The Catholic faith was not as weak as I thought it would be. However, there were differences. Mass was limited to under an hour, and, if it exceeded one hour, the congregation became uncomfortable. I wondered, "How could this be?" Who decided to limit the Mass to one hour? I thought that the sacrifice of the Mass, being the highest sacrifice, should be something in which Catholics participated without counting the minutes. I was concerned about the one hour limitation that seemed to be the norm.

Another surprise I had was the pro-life march that took place from San Jose Catholic Church to the State Capital Building in Austin. Many parishioners from different parts of the Diocese and beyond came, praying the rosary, singing songs to our Blessed Mother, and walking down Congress Street, happy that they were identified with saving human life. The procession of prayer by many parishioners and

Rev. Fr. Evaristus Uche Obikwelu

some non-Catholics reminded me of the processions we had in the Onitsha Archdiocese. Parish priests, bearing the Sacred Eucharist in a monstrance, and parishioners marched to Holy Trinity Cathedral (Basilica now) for the archbishop's final prayer and benediction. Through these similarities, I understood that, even though America had become a secular society, it was not all about pop culture. I identified with the Catholic traditions I knew growing up in Nigeria.

When it came to American English and my British English spoken with a Nigerian Igbo accent -- that was where the rubber met the road. Texans speak their own language – differently from other Americans -- with a twang. They speak slowly. When I bought a soda (soft drink) I was told that my change was a "kwawta". I asked, "What? What is that?" So, the cashier told me that was twenty-five cents. I did not guess it from the way he pronounced quarter. Likewise, when I spoke, I was often asked, "You wanna say that ag'in?" Texans are always "fixin' to go" or "fixin' to leave". I love Texas!

Father David hosted me for about a year. I underwent a psychological test, which felt very strange. I performed domestic activities: cleaning house, doing dishes, mowing the grass, and keeping the courtyard clean. I used public transportation and made adequate use of the State library. Sometimes I took the bus to the Diocesan Chancery and helped stuff envelopes in the Communications Department. I lived in the Borromeo House with Father David about six months

Mary, the Mediatrix of God's Grace

before I met the bishop. At the end of the summer, Father David told me he was satisfied with my adaptation to the culture of the United States and that I would soon meet the bishop.

As I gradually became culturally acquainted with America, Father David became acquainted with my culture and my way of speaking. In Nigeria, a bishop is addressed as "my lord" or "your lordship". So, before I met Bishop Gregory Aymond, Father David told me, "Uche, we address the bishop as 'Bishop'." I agreed to do my best to remember, but habits are sometimes difficult to change. At a social gathering of all the seminarians, the vocation director's team, and the parents and guardians of seminarians, I met the bishop the first time. Father David stepped forward with me and said to the bishop, "Here is Uche, our potential seminarian." Before the bishop could raise his hand to welcome me I said "Good evening, My Lord." Quickly remembering what Father David had told me, I said, "Oh, sorry, good evening, Bishop." Bishop Aymond; with his charismatic smile and in his joyful, welcoming way; looked around, smiling at the seminarians and Father David. He said, "Hey! (If) Uche keeps calling me My Lord, My Lord. I think we're going to accept him."

Formally accepted as a seminarian, I went to Saint Mary Seminary for an interview with the faculty. Although I was accepted, I could not stay for studies with only a tourist visa. So documents were prepared for me by the school and the Diocese of Austin. I returned

Rev. Fr. Evaristus Uche Obikwelu

to Belgium, my domicile at that time, and secured a student visa, from the American Embassy in Brussels.

I was welcomed by Very Reverend Matt Iwuji, who showed me brotherly hospitality when I arrived in Texas. He was the first Nigerian priest I met in Texas, serving as the Judicial Vicar for the Austin Diocese at that time.

I returned to the States and went to Saint Mary's Seminary in Houston, Texas, to study theology for five years. Is it a coincidence that the name of my first and only diocesan theology seminary in the States was named after our Blessed Mother, Saint Mary? I think it was providential. The Virgin Mary knew I was the happiest man ever. Under her watchful eye, I had passed through many tenuous stages before joining the seminary.

Mary, the Mediatrix of God's Grace

CHAPTER 13
Saint Mary Seminary

In the fall of 2004 I began the journey that led to the fulfillment of my covenant with Our Blessed Mother. I considered mine a late vocation because I was already in my mid-thirties. My classmates were mostly in their early twenties. I had mixed feelings about the age difference, but, at the same time, it gave me an opportunity to be patient, which is not one of the easiest virtues in the world. We all began formation to the priesthood. I saw American culture first hand in my fellow seminarians. Likewise, they, too, were able to encounter a culture outside the one in which they were reared. The saying "America is a melting pot" seemed to come alive.

The four pillars of formation: spiritual, intellectual, human, and pastoral and apostolic formation, were very helpful in seminary training. For spiritual formation I was blessed with a very gentle and understanding director, Father Ivan Marsh. He guided me through the easy and the difficult times. Intellectual formation helped harness my potential to articulate the teachings of the Church within the American Catholic Community. Human formation helped me relate to my classmates because the seminarians comprised a microcosm of the macrocosm that is the larger society. Pastoral and apostolic formation dealt with the cultural environment in which I

Rev. Fr. Evaristus Uche Obikwelu

would, eventually, exercise my ministry. Pastoral formation offered the opportunity to seek out and understand situations in which a parishioner might find himself or herself, and a way to offer proper guidance and hope. Likewise, apostolic formation helped me love and appreciate ministry assignments. For example, in a Houston parish, I was assigned to assist in teaching the Rite of Christian Initiation for Adults (RCIA). Also, I was assigned to care for the retired priests at Saint Dominic Center Retirement Home in Houston. These pillars prepared me for ministries after priestly ordination.

During my first year of seminary formation, under the leadership of Very Reverend Brendon Cahill (now Most Reverend Brendon Cahill, the bishop of the Victoria Diocese, Texas), I felt the warmth of a father and pastor. He empathized with both faculty members and seminarians. As rector, he had a greatly positive impact on my formation. I observed, learned, and accepted seminary regulations. My first Formation Director was Msgr. Danny Flores, who was appointed Auxiliary Bishop, and now is the Bishop of Brownsville, Texas. Reverend Michael Olson (now Bishop of Forth Worth Diocese, Texas), taught me moral theology and was a very encouraging friend. Later, Very Reverend Traun Nguyen, the rector now, was my formation director. The faculty at Saint Mary's was amazing.

In my second year I was instituted to the lector ministry, which meant I could read in the church and teach catechism classes. In the same

Mary, the Mediatrix of God's Grace

year I also traveled to Cuernavaca, Mexico, to learn Spanish. During my trip I visited the shrine of the Vergen de Guadalupe (Virgin of Guadalupe), and also saw Saint Juan Diego's Tilma.

After my second year I was assigned to a pastoral year at Saint Mary's Parish in Wimberley, Texas. (In the secular world this is comparable to an internship.) There I put my training into practice in a parish setting. During a prayerful moment, it dawned on me that my first pastoral ministry outside academia was in a church named after Our Blessed Mother, Saint Mary. For me that was another sign that her hand was still on my shoulder.

The Pastoral Advisory Team (PAT) at Saint Mary's was composed of ten members chosen by the pastor, who were commissioned to assist me during my pastoral assignment. Each PAT member submitted critiques of my reflections and made suggestions in areas they felt I needed improvement. They also offered compliments and encouragement. It was a very healthy and helpful experience.

After my pastoral year evaluation by the faculty and the pastor of Saint Mary's in Wimberley, I began my third year of theology at the seminary. The Knights of Columbus Organization blessed me with both financial help and prayers when I returned to the seminary. Of course, the Diocese of Austin supported its seminarians, but the Knights of Columbus made it possible for me to purchase necessary

Rev. Fr. Evaristus Uche Obikwelu

items for my priesthood, like the chasuble for my first Mass in Agulu. Bishop Gregory Aymond ordained seminarians to transitional deacons a year before they became priests, allowing the new deacon to be active in the diocese while still in the seminary. The year allowed the deacon to adjust and assimilate into pastoral work, avoiding culture shock. Some dioceses, who ordained deacons three or six months before priestly ordination, agreed to implement the Austin Diocese's one-year diaconate ordination because it was so successful.

I was ordained to the diaconate ministry on May 17, 2008. As a transitional deacon, Sacred Heart Catholic Church in La Grange was my assignment. I shuttled every other weekend from Saint Mary's Seminary in Houston to La Grange. One great parishioner I encountered was, and still is, my personal physician, Dr. Thomas Borgstedte. He is not only a good Catholic but a perfect gentlemen. From the moment I met him, he and his beautiful family treated me as a family member. He allowed me to call him at any time of the day. He helped me maintain my health in order to serve God's people, not only at La Grange, but in all the parishes I have worked. How many of you have your doctor's cell phone number? I have mine.

Mary, the Mediatrix of God's Grace

CHAPTER 14
Priestly Ordination

I had not seen my parents or siblings since I left for Belgium on September 2, 2002. I was delighted when my sisters, Nne and Ngoo, and my brother, Father Chuks, came to my ordination. During the dinner, organized by Bishop Aymond, in honor of my visiting family, my sister reported that Mom had been asked, "Why had she not been worried and concerned that her last child had left the shores of Nigeria for over seven years, and, still, she never felt the anxiety of a mother to see her son or have her son visit her?" Mom told her friends, "My son went to the States to become a Catholic priest and the Catholic Church is universal. It is the same all over the world. Therefore, I believe he

(Then) Bishop Gregory Aymond of the Austin Diocese ordained Transitional Deacon Uche Obikwelu to the Order of Priesthood

Rev. Fr. Evaristus Uche Obikwelu

is in good hands because he is still in the same church family." Bishop Gregory Aymond was so moved by this testimony from my mom that he included her sentiments in my priestly ordination homily.

Preparing for ordination, especially at the rehearsal, in the presence of my siblings who were in America for the first time, and guests and friends, I told myself, "So it is true that Our Blessed Mother's covenant is about to come to fruition." I had never been a priest before. I did not know what I was about to experience. Would I look different after ordination, or would I no longer have my accent? Or maybe I would not laugh and smile as wide, or talk as loud. I reflected on these and the mystery of ontological change which makes a priest a priest. I prayed as I went to bed on June 5, 2009, and woke up to "D-Day" June 6, 2009. The moment I felt transformed was not when my name was called and the bishop received the request to ordain me a priest. It was not amidst the applause when we candidates turned to the congregation. I felt transformed when I was prostrated on the floor and the litany of saints began to toll. Then I realized that I had died to myself and lived to be configured to Christ. The ordination rite was an amazing experience. At the end of the Mass, after the bishop had introduced the new priests to the entire church, the applause was deafening and almost refused to stop. It was then that I said to myself, "Santa Maria, consumatum est." (Holy Mary, it is finished.)

Mary, the Mediatrix of God's Grace

I became the first indigenous Agulu to be ordained a Roman Catholic Priest in the Diocese of Austin and the United States of America. My maternal cousin, Reverend Nnamdi Moneme was the second in the United States. Reverend Nnamdi is the son of Engineer Paul Moneme and Florence Moneme.

At last, the covenant had come true -- a clear testimony that the Memorare is indeed a reality.

The Memorare

Remember, O most gracious Virgin Mary, that never was it known that anyone who fled to thy protection, implored thy help, or sought thy intercession was left unaided. Inspired with this confidence, I fly to thee, O Virgin of virgins, my Mother; to thee do I come; before thee I stand, sinful and sorrowful. O Mother of the Word Incarnate, despise not my petitions, but in thy mercy hear and answer me. Amen.

Mary, the Mediatrix of God's Grace

CHAPTER 15
Priestly Ministry

Nothing had ever fulfilled me like having my dream and my heart's desire come to fruition. My goal was to plow into active ministry. I was happy to receive my first assignment as parochial vicar at Saint Vincent de Paul Parish in Austin under the pastorship of Reverend Danny Garcia. The wonderful staff and the great parishioners welcomed me like their own son. This was my first experience as a parochial vicar and I was very exuberant and amazed. I enjoyed celebrating the Holy Eucharist, chanting at Mass, visiting and anointing the sick, and visiting and attending different ministries in the parish. Saint Vincent de Paul parishioners distinguished themselves as lovers of

Farewell from Reverend Danny Garcia (now Auxiliary Bishop of Austin) at my goodbye party at Saint Vincent de Paul, 2011

Rev. Fr. Evaristus Uche Obikwelu

priests -- no matter the race, tongue, nationality, or background. It was the epitome of a truly welcoming parish.

I had the privilege of serving in two more parishes as parochial vicar where I acquired some helpful experiences that I continue to use in my ministry.

Diocesan priests have to be with and among the people of the parish.

Fr. Uche blessed the Revised Roman Catholic Missal at Saint Thomas Aquinas, Advent 2012

Priestly ministry, especially diocesan priesthood, is not a corporation. It is the Body of Christ. A priest, as the alter Christus (another Christ), should be Christ to the people. He should be cheerful and welcoming. Although not important to many people, these factors are very essential to an active and effective ministry. I have indeed utilized these gifts successfully and found them helpful.

Somerville, Texas

When a bishop assigns a priest he does not just pluck him from one parish and plant him in another. No, the bishop uses his "Personnel Board" who looks into the qualities, capabilities and pastoral abilities

Mary, the Mediatrix of God's Grace

of priests and then makes recommendations regarding placement of a priest into an effective environment. A priest might be considered for two, three, or more parishes before he is finally assigned. That was my case. I realized that the Virgin Mary's hand still rested on my shoulders when I became the priest in charge of St Ann Catholic Church, Somerville, Texas, and Blessed Virgin Mary Parish in Old Washington on the Brazos, Texas. Upon hearing the names of the parishes it became evident that my first assignment spoke of the Blessed Mother's involvement. I was the priest in charge of a parish named after the grandmother of our Lord, Jesus Christ, and mother of Mary; and a mission parish named after Mary, the mother of Jesus.

(L to R) Deacon Don Sims, Bishop Joe Vasquez, Reverend Father Uche Obikwelu, Deacon Limas Sweed, Taken at Blessed Virgin Mary Parish

 # Rev. Fr. Evaristus Uche Obikwelu

(L to R) Auxiliary Bishop Danny Garcia, Bishop Joe Vasquez, and Reverend Father Uche Obikwelu at the Rural Life Mass

When I reflected on this assignment, Mother Mary's message came back to me, "My son, I am still with you." During the first Sunday homily, I had the courage to share my journey to the priesthood with my parishioners – a journey anchored in my love for Our Blessed Mother. I dedicated my priestly vocation to her. In concluding, I reminded them that it still surprised me that Our Blessed Mother had given me two parishes located in towns I never heard of, and that they were named after her mother and herself. She had a reason for sending me to Somerville, Texas. I think it was providential.

One of the highlights of my ministry in Somerville was to host the 26th Annual Rural Life Mass. The Mass was sponsored by the Saint Ann Council of Catholic Women and the Eastern Council of

Mary, the Mediatrix of God's Grace

Catholic Women. The inspired Mass was celebrated by the Bishop of the Austin Diocese, Joe Vasquez, and his assistant, Auxiliary Bishop Danny Garcia. The event was attended by the spiritual directors of the Catholic Women's Councils from different deaneries, by priests, deacons, religious, and parishioners from the whole diocese. The Fourth Degree Knights of Columbus mounted a guard of honor.

Bishop Vasquez received a special award from incoming president, Karen Pinard

Bishop Vasquez received the offertory

Rev. Fr. Evaristus Uche Obikwelu

Parishioner, Fran Thomas, cracks Father Uche up!

L to R) Deacon Limas Sweed, Reverend Father Uche Obikwelu, and altar server Dalvin Taylor

Mary, the Mediatrix of God's Grace

Rural Life Mass

The congregation

 # Rev. Fr. Evaristus Uche Obikwelu

Mary Knows

As I grew up I observed some non-Catholics' ideas about Our Blessed Mother, the Virgin Mary. However, it worried me that some Catholics, and even a few members of the Catholic clergy, seemed to share in the idea that Catholics worship Mary! There is a phrase in America, "Hello-o-o-o-o!!!" that means "Are you kidding me?" Mary knows she is not a goddess. Our Blessed Mother does not need us to lecture her about humility, which she

Our Lady of Guadalupe statue at Saint Ann Church

already lived. In the Gospel of Luke1:27-31, we were told "And in the sixth month the angel Gabriel was sent from God unto a city of Galilee, named Nazareth, to a virgin espoused to a man whose name was Joseph, of the house of David; and the virgin's name was Mary. And the angel came in unto her, and said, 'Hail, thou that art highly favored; the Lord is with thee: blessed art thou among women.' And when she saw him, she was troubled at his saying, and cast in her

Mary, the Mediatrix of God's Grace

mind what manner of salutation this should be. And the angel said unto her, 'Fear not, Mary: for thou hast found favor with God. And, behold, thou shalt conceive in thy womb, and bring forth a son, and shalt call his name JESUS'." Mary's "Fiat" spoke every truth.

I was indeed jolted when a Catholic confronted me, saying that thousands of people embark on a pilgrimage to Mexico to worship Mary at the shrine of the Virgin of the Guadalupe, while the Churches are not full. He meant that more people went there to worship her than went to worship at Mass. I shall address that misconception, as well as others held by non-Catholics. God never consulted any other human being before He sent the Angel Gabriel to Mary. There was no evidence that Mary was aware that the Angel Gabriel was to visit her, nor did she show any sign that she was ambitious. Mary manifested the noble simplicity of an innocent heart in a young daughter of Abraham. That is why, in her most noble simplicity, she replied to the message of the Angel, "Let it be done according to your Will."

At Cana, during His first public miracle, Mary innocently asked Jesus' favor for wine to save the new couple from embarrassment. Her Son, reminded her that His time had not come yet for such a miracle. She humbly left, but still, respectfully, went to the servants and told them to do whatever He asked. Now, pay attention. Mary did not feel ashamed like we would have felt; she did not go about

 **Rev. Fr. Evaristus Uche Obikwelu**

complaining or pouting. No! Why? Because Mary knew she was the handmaid of God. She is not God. She is not a goddess. She knows she is God's daughter and, by God's grace and privilege, also God's Mother. So, when anybody tries to insinuate that Catholics worship Mary they should reflect again her actions at Cana.

By the Holy Sacrifice of the Mass, Catholics offer the Highest Sacrifice to God through Our Lord Jesus by the hands of the priest. The Council of Ephesus, 431 AD, said that God visited us at the Incarnation when He chose Mary to be Theotokos (God bearer). It is, therefore, proper that we ask Mary, who found favor in the sight of God, to help us receive grace from God. That is why I made a covenant with her to be a member of her Son's priesthood. It is my privilege to serve in that capacity now.

In my first Masses after ordination, both in the United States and in Nigeria, and sometimes in other parishes where I served, I asked people when they thought we should get tired of asking for the intercession of Our Blessed Mother, the Virgin Mary, and leave the Catholic Church for a non-Catholic denomination. The answer is NEVER!

Mary, the Mediatrix of God's Grace

Mary's ageless grotto at Saint Ann Catholic Church, Somerville, TX

Mary, the Mediatrix of God's Grace

Part IV:
THE BLASPHEMY
OF OUR TIME

Mary, the Mediatrix of God's Grace

CHAPTER 16
The Havoc of Mary's Blasphemy

On March 8, 2017, the world celebrated Women's Day - a day when the world highlights the importance and value of women in our world. Everybody knows that every human being born in this world was born of a woman. Therefore, it is appropriate that we should celebrate and honor our women. Having said that, I must suggest that the celebration of women should not stop only at fanfare, marches, speeches and all kinds of activisms, but should go further to showcase the true value of what women really represent. Coming from the Catholic perspective, it is very clear that Our Blessed Mother, the Virgin Mary, represents in every ramification the true woman for all women, not because we gave her this honor or these privileges, but because God Himself gave them to her. When it was time for Him to begin the economy of salvation for mankind - to redeem man from the original sin and the eternal damnation that our fore parents, Adam and Eve, got us into, - He sent His Archangel Gabriel to a young Lady in Israel, Mary the daughter of Zion; the daughter of Anne and Joachim. This very gesture, as I have already indicated in this book, presents Mary as a favorite to God. So, if God chose her it is necessary that we, God's creatures, should follow suit to honor her.

Sadly, as the Women's March was under way, some women decided

 **Rev. Fr. Evaristus Uche Obikwelu**

to use this particular day, (which should have been a day to honor women,) for their personal ego, political agenda, and material gains. In Argentina, for example we read as well as watched pictures on the internet where some women blasphemed against the Mother of God by depicting her as an abortionist. The image of a pregnant Mary standing with a bloody fetus at her feet was gruesome, despicable and blasphemous. (https://cruxnow.com/global-church/2017/03/10/argentinas-march-women-became-attack-church/). That is why I captioned this chapter the "The Havoc of Mary's Blasphemy." This is a tragedy of our time. On many occasions, we have read and also heard different kinds of mockery and unjustifiable jokes by comedians, musicians, and actors against the Virgin Mary, and they serve to demonstrate how our secular world has accepted abnormalities as normal. This type of attitude is not only observed or noticed within the secular world, but unfortunately, is found among Christians and even among members of the clergy. It is a known fact that Catholics do not worship Mary, but they honor her because she followed in the footsteps of God. Despite this reality, some Christians—both Catholics and non-Catholics—have denigrated the Virgin Mary as just an instrument that conveyed the Savior; therefore, she should not be given such prominent recognitions.

Understandably, it has been proven that when we blaspheme or caricature or denigrate holy things, especially in the realm of the Divine, such denigration often is accompanied by certain calamities.

Mary, the Mediatrix of God's Grace

Those who tried it, as well as their friends and relatives, knew what happened to them. Although this happens sparingly in our present time, no one is justified in engaging or indulging in such disrespectful behaviors towards sacred things. The Virgin Mary has appeared in many parts of the world: The Lady of Fatima apparition; Our Lady of Guadalupe; our Lady of Lourdes; and many others that need not be mentioned here. However, one significant factor that calls for examination here is that at every apparition, Our Blessed Mother always directs attention to her Son, Our Lord Jesus Christ. The emphasis is never on her. The Holy Mother Church has rigorously examined all these apparitions according to required Church regulations, and approved them as worthy of belief; despite this fact, many still have doubts, but their doubts do not nullify the truth of the apparitions. It is very sad when people in our secular society commit blasphemy by going out of their way to denigrate Our Blessed Mother just to make a political or entertainment point. We should be witnesses of our Faith in our world today. Of course, we know that not all religions will be patient with such scandalous attitudes against a revered one in their religion. However, when we Catholics and some Christians see the humiliation being given to Our Blessed Mother, our hearts bleed. Instead of becoming violent, we take it to prayer, we speak up, and we try to educate either by dialoging directly or writing up a piece. Interestingly, many of the critics of Our Blessed Mother (such as high-profile female musicians) received their basic education from nuns and priests in Catholic primary and

Rev. Fr. Evaristus Uche Obikwelu

high schools. Some even completed special classes in the Catholic Church called religious education (RE), but after graduating from the university, and moving into the workforce with the ability to provide for themselves, they decided to turn away from the faith that nurtured them. Isn't that very sad?

Close at home, why do some Catholics and other Christians have a problem with the visitation to the sites of apparitions of Our Blessed Mother around the world? Why do they have problems praying the rosary, which was given to us by Our Blessed Mother through the three visionaries at the apparition of Fatima? Many of these people complain that the faithful go to these sites claiming to receive God's grace and blessings through the Virgin Mary. This practice seems to be a big headache for them. They would prefer that we stay at home and do not give Mary those recognitions because for them, it is tantamount to worshiping her. My response to those Catholics and other Christians who have problems with this act of religious piety is to humble themselves enough to ask, "Why do I have a problem with the gift that God has given to humanity?" In all her apparitions, has Mary ever condemned anybody who did not honor her? She has always spoken for the good of humanity, irrespective of religion. When she spoke at Fatima, she spoke against the evil of communism, and requested that we pray the rosary so that mankind can be saved from the calamity that was to happen. Again, she spoke about the first and second World Wars, and asked us to pray so that

Mary, the Mediatrix of God's Grace

humanity would be saved from such dangerous outcomes of the war. She was never perturbed by the neglect or the shameful disgrace in which some individuals indulged.

Mary, the Mediatrix of God's Grace

CHAPTER 17
Mary Versus World Celebrities

As we mentioned in our earlier chapter, many high-profile politicians, musicians, actors and actresses, have on many occasions come out against the teachings of the Church. Why? Because they are openly against the teachings of the Church. Here, we speak about certain fundamental moral teachings of the church, for example, marriage only between a man and a woman (Genesis 5:2). Instead, proponents of abortion encourage anti-religious liberty bills and laws designed to force the Church to perform certain functions against their teachings. All these go to show the arrogance and secularist spirit of our celebrities, who received their talents and gifts and positions in the society from God, not from their own personal efforts only, as they might think. Based on the above discussion, it is very sad that in most Christian countries of the world, especially in Europe and North America, all references to God and Mary have been removed from society (e.g. schools, public buildings, etc,). Suffice it to say that the effort to subject ourselves to the principles of secularism and radical globalism is a clear attempt to deny God and His prominent presence in our lives and in our world. The danger of the arrogance of the celebrities is that the world today listens to them as the conveyors of the truth. However, what the world sees as truth from them is not really the "Truth" but a personal opinion that has found comfort in

Rev. Fr. Evaristus Uche Obikwelu

the minds of a few that believe the same way they believe. Some of our children watch movies, listen to the music of musicians, and come to believe that success in their professions must be evidence that such sources are correct in what they say, which is a flat lie. Likewise, our world politicians have arrogated to themselves the right to teach, the right to determine what is true or false, the right to make laws that most often go against morality. This gesture is not only the height of arrogance, but is a tragedy for the world that is in need of God's mercy.

My suggestion is that all people of the world, no matter their positions in society, should realize the humbleness of the Mother of God, a young girl who accepted God's will to carry His child, despite the fact that she did not understand how that mystery was to pan out. This woman is a role model, not only for the world, but especially for women. Mary has shown us in many aspects that the best way for us to solve our problems and live our lives honestly on this earth is to hold tight to the Holy Eucharist of the Mass and the rosary. Thus, we will enjoy eternal bliss with God in heaven. One may ask me, "Father, how about the non-Catholics and non-Christians?" I will respond that God created all human beings; and the Second Vatican Council in Lumen Gentium, (The Light of the World) suggests to us that "God is the creator of all and invites everyone to live according to the will of God." By this suggestion, the Council makes clear that men and women, in their different states of life, are called to live life that

Mary, the Mediatrix of God's Grace

is worthy of God's grace. Having accepted the above premise, it is very clear that the Church does not now judge that only those who go to Mass or say the rosary will inherit the Kingdom, but others who live their daily lives according to the mind of God. Nevertheless, our Blessed Mother, the Virgin Mary, has instructed us, her children, to always attend Mass and pray the rosary. It is our privilege to follow these instructions which will bring us closer to God.

Finally, it is incumbent on our world celebrities to emulate the humility that is embodied in the Mother of God, and instead of engaging in sacrilegious speeches and disrespectful activisms against her, they should become her disciples.

Mary, the Mediatrix of God's Grace

CHAPTER 18
The Silence of Goodwill

The Irish philosopher, Edmund Burke, said, "All that is necessary for the triumph of evil is that good men do nothing." Today the quote of Edmund Burke is as relevant as it was about a century ago. From our discussion so far, it is very clear that many views and opinions that have been expressed against the Church and Our Blessed Virgin Mary have remained either unchallenged or ignored. Why? Because the world today prefers to sacrifice sacredness on the altar of political correctness. On many occasions, people speak in a very disrespectful and condescending manner when the topic is on God, His Son, Jesus Christ, the Holy Spirit, Our Blessed Mother and the Church without any concern that they are committing a blasphemy. On the other hand, when the topic is politicians, celebrities of many kinds, and other mere creatures, they speak glowingly about them. Isn't this unimaginable? The sadness here is not about the ignorance of these people, but the deliberate intention to control the worldview narrative. This brings me to the point about complacency in the face of blasphemy against the Virgin Mary. How many Catholics, non-Christian religious and, members of the clergy have stood up against such groups that indulge in this kind of blasphemy? Many fear the loss of members of their congregations, others are concerned how they will be perceived by the public, still others are worried about

being alienated by their family and friends who might accuse them of being "holier than thou." This is where Burke's message is more important than ever because, for evil and blasphemy against the holy ones to thrive, we must be silent. Men and women of goodwill will work hard to avoid this temptation.

It is based on Burke's principle, and faith in the Catholic Church, that I have chosen to respond to those who take the mercy of God for granted by indulging in blasphemy because, if I do not speak up, I could be perceived as explicitly endorsing their actions. Therefore, I must categorically state that all kinds of atrocities, condescending remarks in speeches, and disrespectful attitudes towards our Blessed Mother are both unacceptable and sacrilegious.

Mary, the Mediatrix of God's Grace

CHAPTER 19

100 Years of Fatima Apparition

Are we not so blessed that it is in our own contemporary era that the Holy Mother Church celebrated the Marian Centennial of the apparition of Our Lady of Fatima, Portugal? On Saturday, May 13, 2017, our Holy Father, Pope Francis, went to Fatima, the site of the apparition, and canonized two of the three visionaries: Saint Jacinta and Saint Francisco. This is a great time in our history because many of us have been able to visit the site of this apparition and some of us have also read about it. One of the visionaries, Lucia, died early in the millennia 2000.

Since the Universal Mother Church is global, we in this part of the world also participated in this historic day. Friends and visitors of Saint Charles Borromeo Catholic Church, Kingsland, Texas and Our Lady of the Lake, Sunrise Beach, Texas honored the hundred-year anniversary of the Fatima apparition with the holy rosary, Holy Eucharist of the Mass and the honorable recitation of the Litany of the Blessed Virgin Mary. These prayers were then followed with a procession by God's lovely people to the statue of our Blessed Mother situated on the grounds of Saint Charles Borromeo. A beautiful rose bouquet was placed at Our Lady's feet. Below, the pictures of this once-in-a-lifetime event speak for themselves.

 # Rev. Fr. Evaristus Uche Obikwelu

The Saint Charles Borromeo Catholic Church, Kingsland, TX, gets ready for the Fatima's Centenary

Father Uche Explains the Special Event of the Day at Mass

Mary, the Mediatrix of God's Grace

Father Uche Pauses Before the Collect (Opening Prayer)

Father Uche gives Homily on the Centenary of Fatima

Rev. Fr. Evaristus Uche Obikwelu

Father Uche holds up the Rosary as He Delivers the Centenary Homily

Father Uche at his Homily

Mary, the Mediatrix of God's Grace

Father Uche Emphasizes the Importance of the Rosary

The Epiclesis (The Descent of the Holy Spirit on the Oblation)

 # Rev. Fr. Evaristus Uche Obikwelu

Blesses the Oblation After the Epiclesis

During the Consecration at the Fatima Centenary Mass

Mary, the Mediatrix of God's Grace

Father Uche Incenses both the Paschal Candle and Our Blessed Mother

Father Uche Leads the Congregation on the Recitation of the Litany of the Blessed Virgin Mary

Rev. Fr. Evaristus Uche Obikwelu

Moves to present the Flower to the Mother of God

The Joyful Congregation Moves with Father Uche to the Shrine Of Mary

Mary, the Mediatrix of God's Grace

The Altar Server Leads with the Incense to the Marian Shrine

Father Uche Pays Homage to the Blessed Mother before he Presents Her the Flowers

Rev. Fr. Evaristus Uche Obikwelu

Father Uche Incenses the Virgin Mary Shrine

Father Uche Leads the Congregation in Veneration of Mary

Mary, the Mediatrix of God's Grace

Congregation that Honors Mary on the Centenary Day of Fatima – May 13, 2017

Father Uche Offers God's Blessing to Gloria J. Hoffman
(Mother of Roger Woods)

 # Rev. Fr. Evaristus Uche Obikwelu

Father Uche Incenses the Virgin Mary Shrine

Mary, the Mediatrix of God's Grace

People from the Neighboring Parishes Participated in this Historic Day

Father Uche Prays for the People and Blesses the Rosaries Presented to Him

 # Rev. Fr. Evaristus Uche Obikwelu

Father Uche and the Altar Server, Louis

Mary, the Mediatrix of God's Grace

Reverend Father Evaristus Uche Obikwelu (Pastor, Saint Charles Borromeo Catholic Church, Kingsland, Tx, and Our Lady of the Lake Mission, Sunrise Beach, TX.) May 13, 2017

Mary, the Mediatrix of God's Grace

CHAPTER 20
The Mother of God Still Stands Tall

Despite all caricatures and sacrilegious behaviors against Our Blessed Mother, the Mother of God still stands tall. I have come to realize that most people have received different kinds of graces, blessings, and miracles from God through the Blessed Virgin Mary, but it seems that a few are embarrassed either to share it or give testimony to it. It is very important for us to accept the reality that miracles in our lives today do not really mean that a blind man must see or a physically challenged person must walk. No, there are many miracles going on daily in our lives and it is incumbent on us Christians, especially Catholics, to witness any miracle that we have received from God, especially through our Blessed Mother, the Virgin Mary. Having shared in this book how the Virgin Mary, in a covenant with me, received from her Son my vocation to the priesthood all the way from Nigeria to America, I would humbly wish to share with you that the Mother of God's hand is still on my shoulder.

I have been a patient of panic attack for some years. Those who have experienced panic attacks know what I am talking about, and those who have not experienced them would never wish to do so. I received treatment and followed the proper therapy, and I continue to follow the doctor's advice, but does this mean that the anxiety has

Rev. Fr. Evaristus Uche Obikwelu

absolutely disappeared? No. Once in a while it resurfaces, but with the knowledge of the therapy required, I respond to it accordingly and get it under control. There is no doubt that many who have suffered with this particular serious ailment also experience difficulties in their professions. After I was transferred to my new assignment, this sad situation continued to show itself periodically despite the fact that I was responding and honoring the advice of medical experts. Finally, it came to the point that my boisterous presence and feisty homilies became subdued to a quiet presence and low tones. Many began to worry: "This is not the Father Uche we know." Tongues began to wag; people were wondering, "What has gotten into Father Uche?" Sometimes when I attended both social and liturgical events, it was evident that the man of exuberance had been reduced to the man of silence -:). Then one day at Mass, after the talk had made it around the community about the change in my demeanor, I decided that it was time to let people know that whatever is going on with me is what happens to us mortals and that I am absolutely taking care of my health to the best of my ability for the good of our ministry of Christ. I asked them for one thing: Do not pity me, but please pray the rosary always for me. By this request, I had absolute confidence that our Blessed Mother would carry my request and the care of God's people to her Son and it would be answered.

Two weeks after this request was made, I was still not being the Father Uche they were used to, so when Mass was over, I went to

Mary, the Mediatrix of God's Grace

the rectory to take some rest hoping that nobody would disturb me, but I was wrong. Good people always seek for the good of priests. A middle-aged man, who is a dentist, sent me a text on my phone (I could barely remember him because I was new to the parish,). In the text he said, "Father, could I see you?" I looked at the text several times; I had no energy to have a long conversation. I was concerned that if I accepted this request I might not be at my best for social interaction. However, as a priest, I believe that we can always do our best to listen to our parishioners. I said to myself, "I will tell him that I have only a few minutes," but the conversation eventually lasted about an hour. When the conversation began, my friend, the dentist, Dr. Clarence Feller, Jr. (a prominent dentist in San Antonio, Texas) said to me, "Father, I am troubled that you are not feeling well. I am concerned because the feistiness of Father Uche's homily has disappeared." This temporarily brought a smile to my face and his too. After our conversation, he recommended that I have a CT scan of my teeth; I wondered what this test could have to do with my anxiety, but I have to trust God and trust the good intentions of my friend and generous Doctor. The CT scan was taken, and amazingly, three root canals were found to be infected and my doctor exclaimed at that moment, "Thank God, I have gotten what I'm looking for." As for me, I was still wondering what this was all about because I have been satisfied for over seven years that my teeth, and my gums are in a very healthy condition. Eventually, I received treatment and the impact of the infection in my body began to subside. Everybody

knows that when a pre-diabetic or a diabetic person has an infection in the blood, the situation is very deadly. Although my doctor didn't want to frighten me, he mildly suggested that it is not good to have a blood infection. I will humbly submit that, since this treatment took place, and the infection has been taken care of, many related problems have improved.

I know that many may still be in doubt about this story, but that is not my problem. The point is that, for years, I did not know that I had these potentially deadly tooth infections, but they provided a good reason for my anxiety attack. I have the belief that when I became very sick, and the treatment for my anxiety didn't seem to be helping, I requested the intercession of Our Blessed Virgin Mary through my parishioners who were concerned about my health and she indeed came to my rescue. Now, my dear friends, if I could not discover this problem before and later it was discovered after this appeal was made (many people testified they prayed rosaries for me), then why should I not honestly acknowledge that this particular grace was granted me by God through our Blessed Mother? We must be ready and courageous to share our testimonies of Divine intervention in our lives; that is one of the ways the world will appreciate God's presence in the world. Finally, the Virgin Mary still stands tall.

Mary, the Mediatrix of God's Grace

ACKNOWLEDGMENTS

Glory to the Most Holy Trinity, thanks to the Mother of God, the Blessed Virgin Mary, my late Dad, Pius Ifem Obikwelu, my Mom, Georgina Udenwa Obikwelu, Bishop Joe S. Vasquez, Auxiliary Bishop Daniel Garcia, Francis Cardinal Arinze, Archbishop Gregory Aymond, Bishop Mike Sis, Bishop Danny Flores, Bishop Brendan Cahill, Bishop Michael Olson, Reverend Fr. Dr. Polycarp Chuks Obikwelu, Reverend Fr. Dr. Eugene Anowai, Very Reverend Matt Iwuji, Archbishop Valerian Okeke, Reverend Fr. Dr. Theophilus Okere, Prof. Fidelis Uzochukwu Okafor

My Siblings: Ilo Obikwelu, Nne Okwoli, Barr. Ify Umeadi-Ajagu, Late Ndu Obikwelu, Hon. Ngoo Nnezianya.

Reverend James Ekeocha, Reverend Pedro Garcia, Reverend Vincent Anyama, Reverend Edwin Kagoo, Reverend Uche Andeh, Reverend Augustine Ariwado, Reverend James Misko, Reverend Reginald Samuels, Reverend Anthony Nwuda, Reverend Fr. Dr. Jude Uwalaka, Reverend Fr. Dr. Clement Obielu, Reverend Traun Nguyen, Prince Kanu, Cyriacus Uche Emebo, Nkem Anih, Kembo Zunzanyika, Ifeanyi Okeke, Will Kapavik, Reverend Basil Aguzi

Peachie Burlin, Shane McCue, Josie Klypas, Maggie Orozco,

Rev. Fr. Evaristus Uche Obikwelu

Deacon Don Sims, Jeff Paradawski, Louise McKenny, Debbie and Jim Juhlke, David McMillan, Dr. Thomas Borgstedte, Reverend Fr. Dr. Emmanuel Umezinwa, Reverend Fr. Dr. Jude Onedunne, Father Gabriel Okoye, Chinyere Lulu Obiorah, Pam Marvin, Dennis Macha, Father Nnamdi Moneme, Kaye Crawford, Reverend Sr. Chika Ezenwabachili, Chief and Mrs. Emmanuel Nwakanwa, Vincent Matocha, Bob Schwab, Betsy Watson.

All the teachers and professors, who have taught me all my school life, to everyone I have encountered in my life, I thank you for any impact you may have made on me. To you all, I remain most grateful. God bless you all! Amen.

Mary, the Mediatrix of God's Grace

READER'S COMMENTS

"It is clear to me after reading about the life journey of Fr Uche Obikwelu, God was indeed inviting him to not only listen, but to follow him! Through the Blessed Mother's intercession, she continually invited Fr. Uche to trust God's ways, which are not always our ways."

   - Most Reverend Daniel Garcia

    Auxiliary Bishop of Austin Diocese

"I read the autobiography with great interest. It is indeed enriching. Father Uche gave a great insight into the Obikwelu Family. The climax of the work is his encounter with our Blessed Mother Mary, through whose intercession he is a priest of God today. I commend Father Uche E. Obikwelu for this wonderful work, which is mainly an act of appreciation to the Blessed Virgin Mary for interceding on his behalf."

   - Reverend Fr. Dr. Poly Chuks Obikwelu

"One of the highlights of a pilgrimage is always the story of the priest's life and vocation. Every vocation story is a unique window into the heart of God and the response of a man with a heart for God. Father Uche's story is right up there with the best. Recalling his Catholic family life in Nigeria and how God spoke to his heart and called him to the priesthood will take you out of your routine to another land and culture. It is not only a spiritually uplifting story, but also an adventure, a biography and a glimpse into the mind of God."

   - SteveRayCatholicConvert.com

Rev. Fr. Evaristus Uche Obikwelu

"I have been truly inspired to deepen my relationship with Our Blessed Mother after reading Father Uche's life story in Mary, the Mediatrix of God's Grace! I do believe that it is Mary's hand that has brought Father Uche to be the new Spiritual Director for our RED-C Apostolate. It is also no coincidence that we have been recently inspired to consecrate our RED-C Catholic Radio to Jesus through Mary. I am looking forward to the many graces that Mary will provide through Father Uche's humble guidance and service!"
   - Dennis Macha, President, RED-C Catholic Radio

"This is a great insight into Father Uche's faith formation and becoming a priest! I enjoyed the read. It flowed well and made good use of historical accounts, relating Catholic formation in Nigeria and in the author."
   - Dr. Thomas Borgstedte

Father's Autobiography is a fascinating look at both Nigerian history and his own, intertwined in a delightful read. Every Nigerian child should have one.
   - Pam Marvin, Radio Host
     Red C Round Up, KEDC

"Father Uche's autobiography is an interestingly written account of his life journey. The struggles he endured with regard to his calling and his covenant with the Blessed Virgin Mary demonstrate the intensity of his religious vocation. Mary, The Mediatrix of God's Grace, provides a window to a culture quite different from ours and to the process of

Mary, the Mediatrix of God's Grace

achieving ordination despite very different circumstances. I found it highly engaging."
- Karen Pinard, President
Austin Diocesan Council of Catholic Women 2016-2017

Father Uche has given all of us a beautiful testimony of Marian devotion. This book is a must read for anyone with a special love of the Blessed Mother… and a must read for anyone who has doubted the power of her intercession.
- Kaye Crawford
Founder, Black Catholic History

I have read the work. As a classmate from our school days, I know about Father Uche's love and respect for history. But this is a story with a universe of difference. It is a personal journey of faith with so many stops, capable of inspiring anyone who will dare to read. This can only come from a true son of Our Lady."
- Reverend Fr. Dr. Emmanuel Umezinwa

"Father Uche poured out his heart in this autobiography. He is a man of great spirituality, with a rare reverence for his Lord and the Blessed Mother. In this work he allows the reader to peek into his depths, revealing his joys and fears."
- Dr. Peachie Burlin,
St. Ann Catholic Church, Somerville TX

Rev. Fr. Evaristus Uche Obikwelu

"In our times of global violence and attack on traditional family and human life, when God appears to be distant from us, Father Uche's book reminds us of one simple fact - God is present and acting in our world and Mother Mary is there to help us embrace God's plan for each of us and for our world. A good read for those who want to find inner peace in a troubled world by imitating the fiat of Mary, 'Behold the handmaid of the Lord, be it be done to me according to thy word'."

   - Reverend Nnamdi Moneme (OMV)

"A vision of our life's history through the prism of faith, reveals what is most true about us. Fr. Uche's Autobiography, which bares the depths of his spiritual core, is a window into what is most true about him: a man of faith and a priest of Christ with a deeply Marian heart."

   - Reverend Vincent Anyama
   Diocese of Dallas

"This book is a witness to what Fr. Uche's spiritual devotion to our Blessed Mother is and of course a source of inspiration to many. He has shown his dedication and commitment over the years to honor his covenant he made with the Mother of God, which ultimately have led to his becoming a Priest."

   - Debbie Juhlke
   Civitan International President

Mary, the Mediatrix of God's Grace

"In this autobiography, Father Uche speaks with refreshing candor, and calls us to notice the every-day miracles that we too easily ignore or explain away. He skillfully relates the spiritual with the material world; we are challenged to see that the Catholic Church, and especially Our Blessed Mother, are under attack, and we ignore it at our peril. Father Uche truly is one of Mary's chosen sons, and is an inspiration to us all."

-Betsy Watson,
Saint Charles Borromeo Church, Kingsland TX

www.ingramcontent.com/pod-product-compliance
Lightning Source LLC
Chambersburg PA
CBHW041630220426
43665CB00001B/6